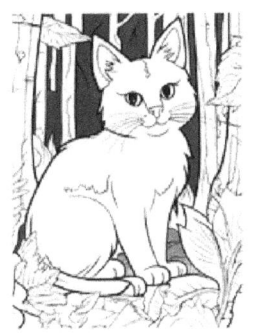

This Book Belongs to

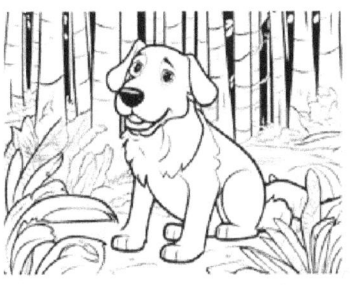

All Reghts Reserved

2024

No part of this publicação be reproduced, distributed or transmitted in photocopying, recording or other electronic or mechanical methods, withour the prior written permission of the publisher, excepcional for brief quotations incorporated in critical reviews and other specific non comercial uses. Any unauthorized réplica of this work is prohibited.

V.A.P.
vanderlea alves publications

Test to color

Vanderlea Alves Publications

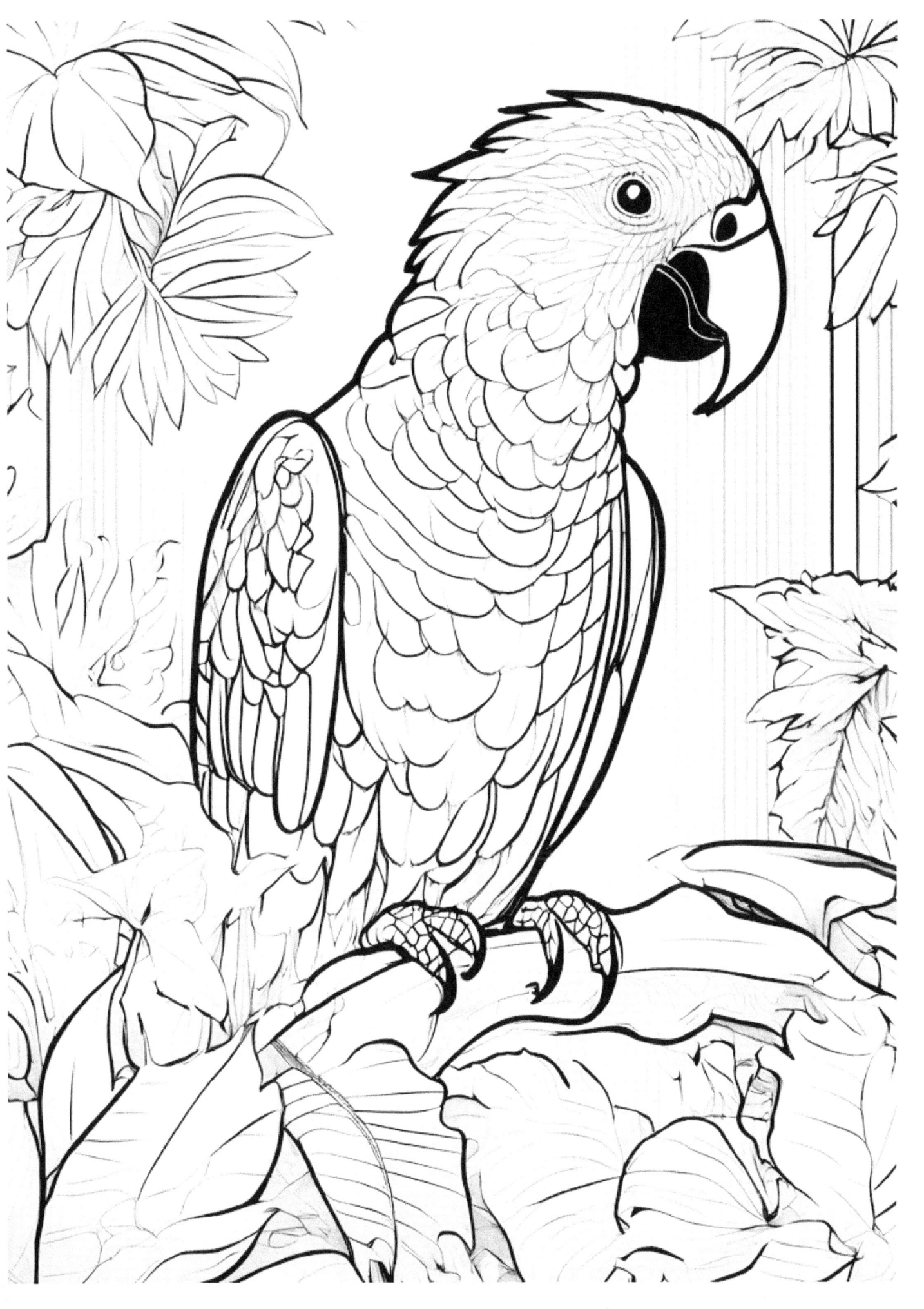

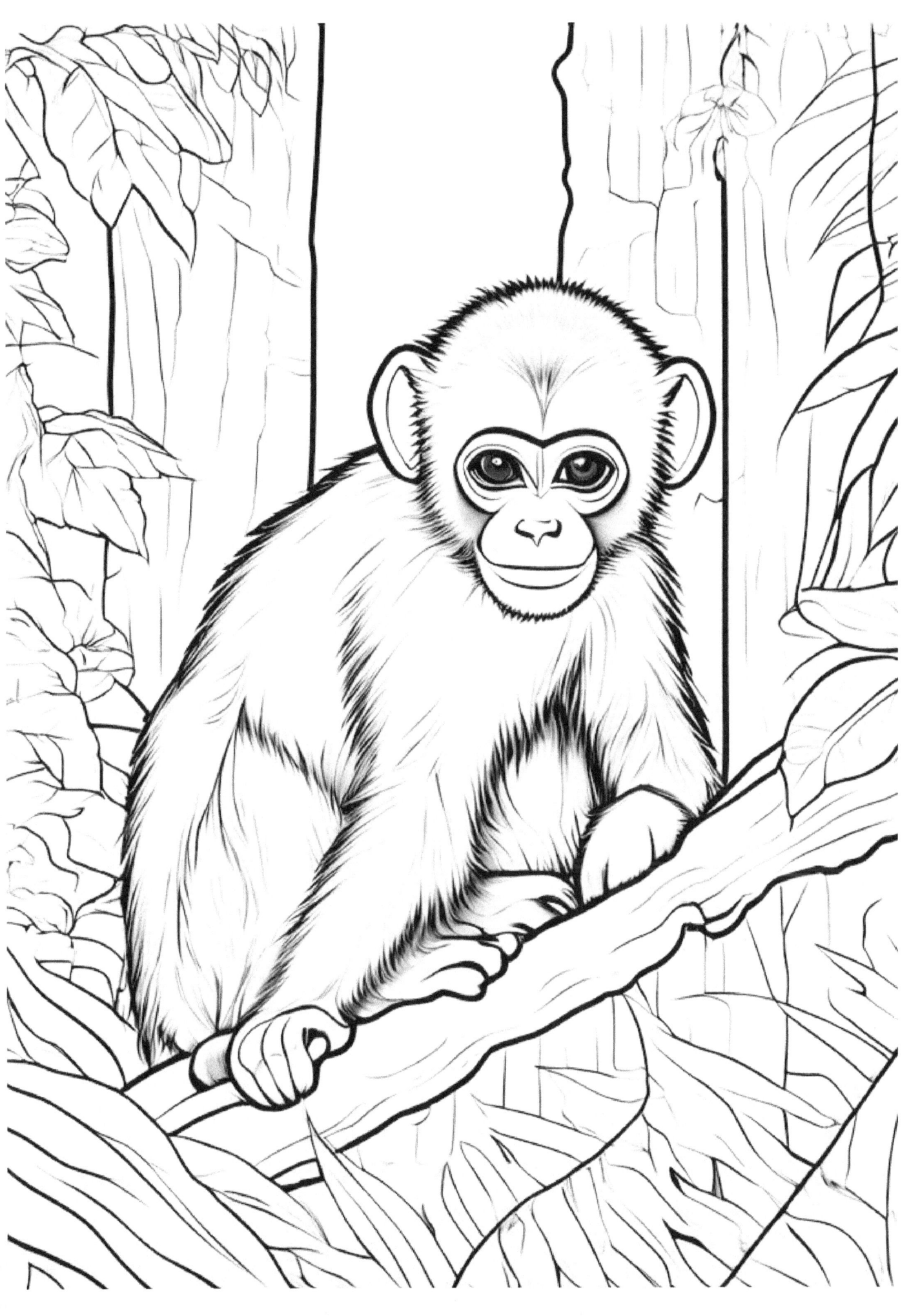

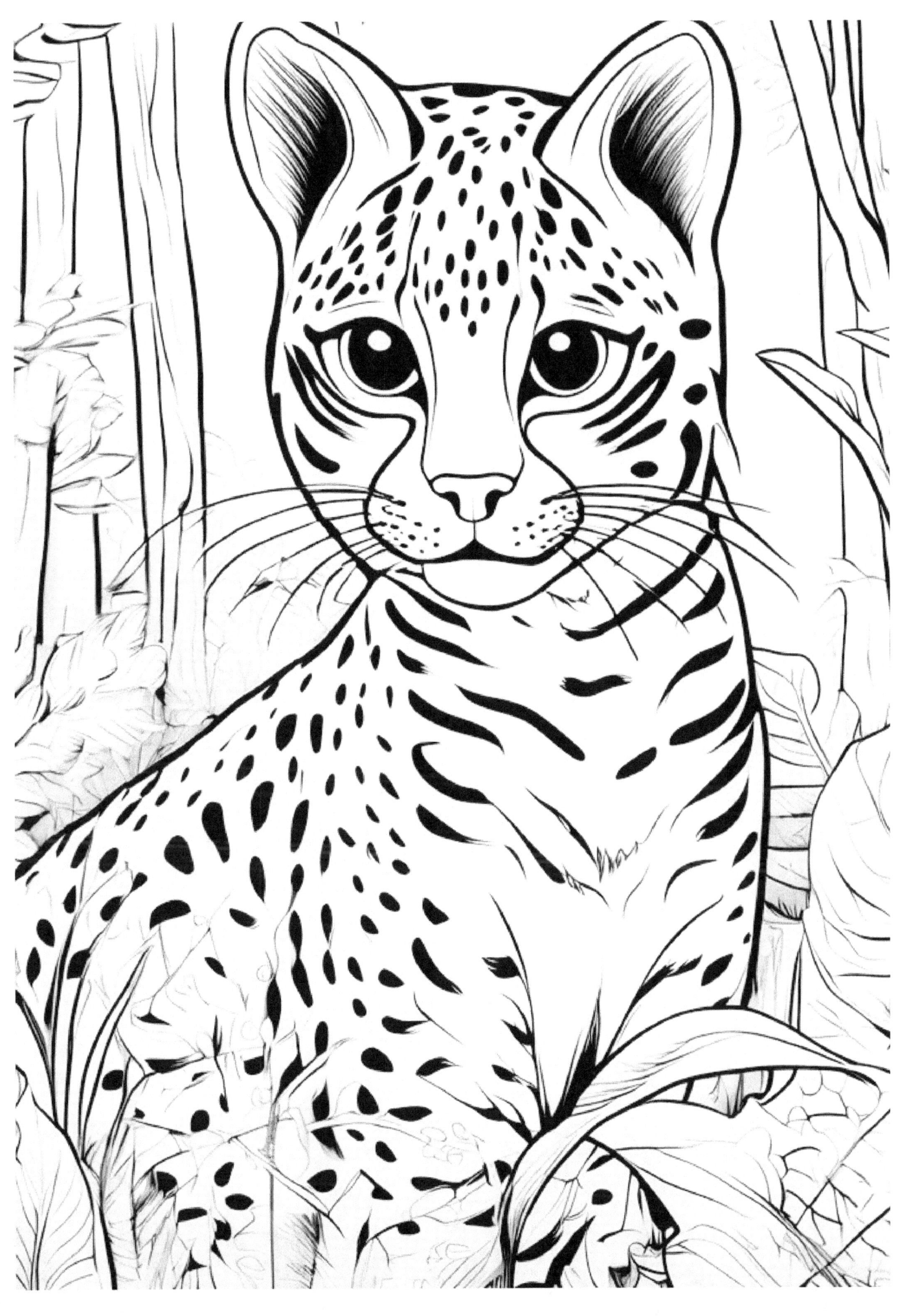

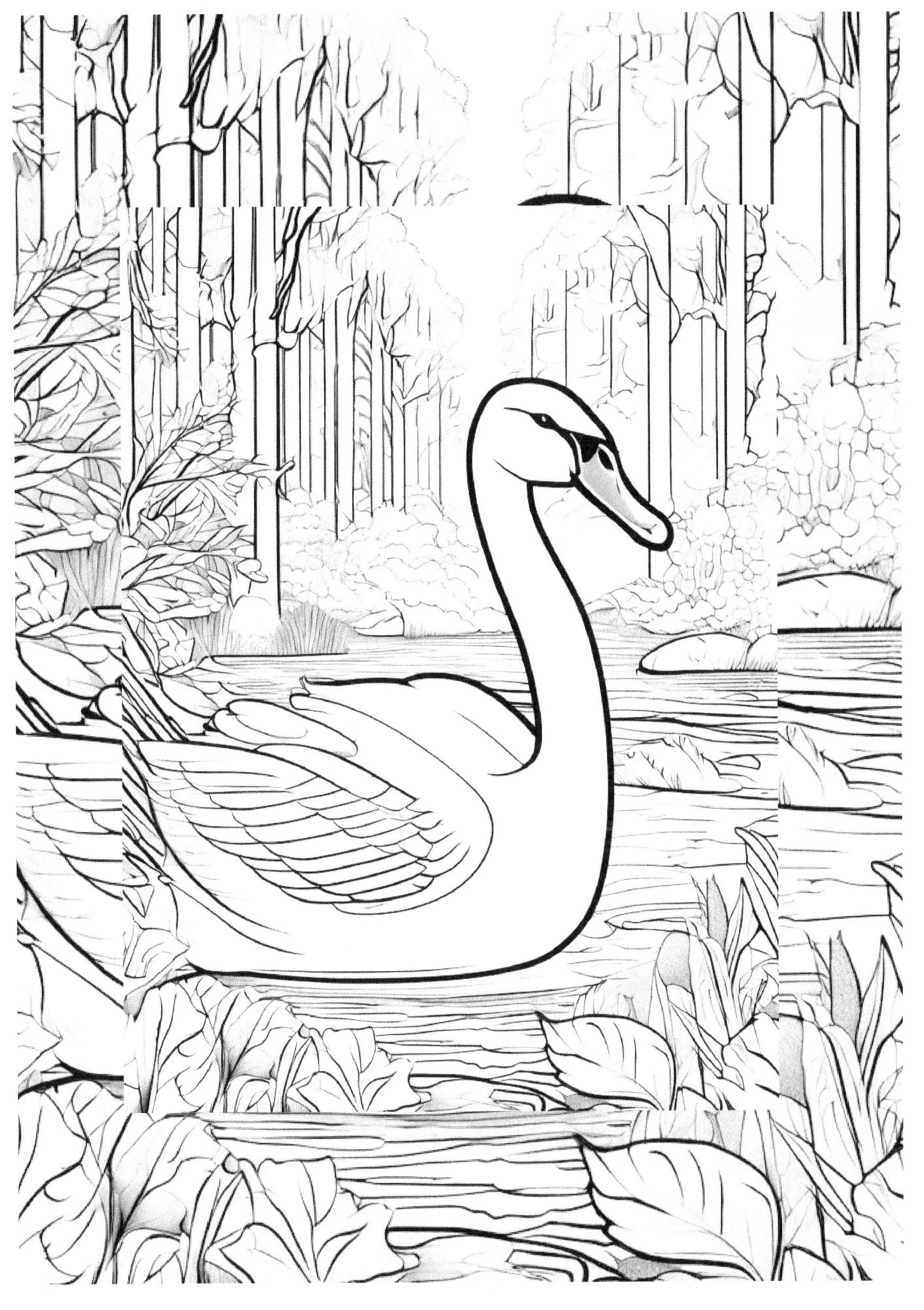

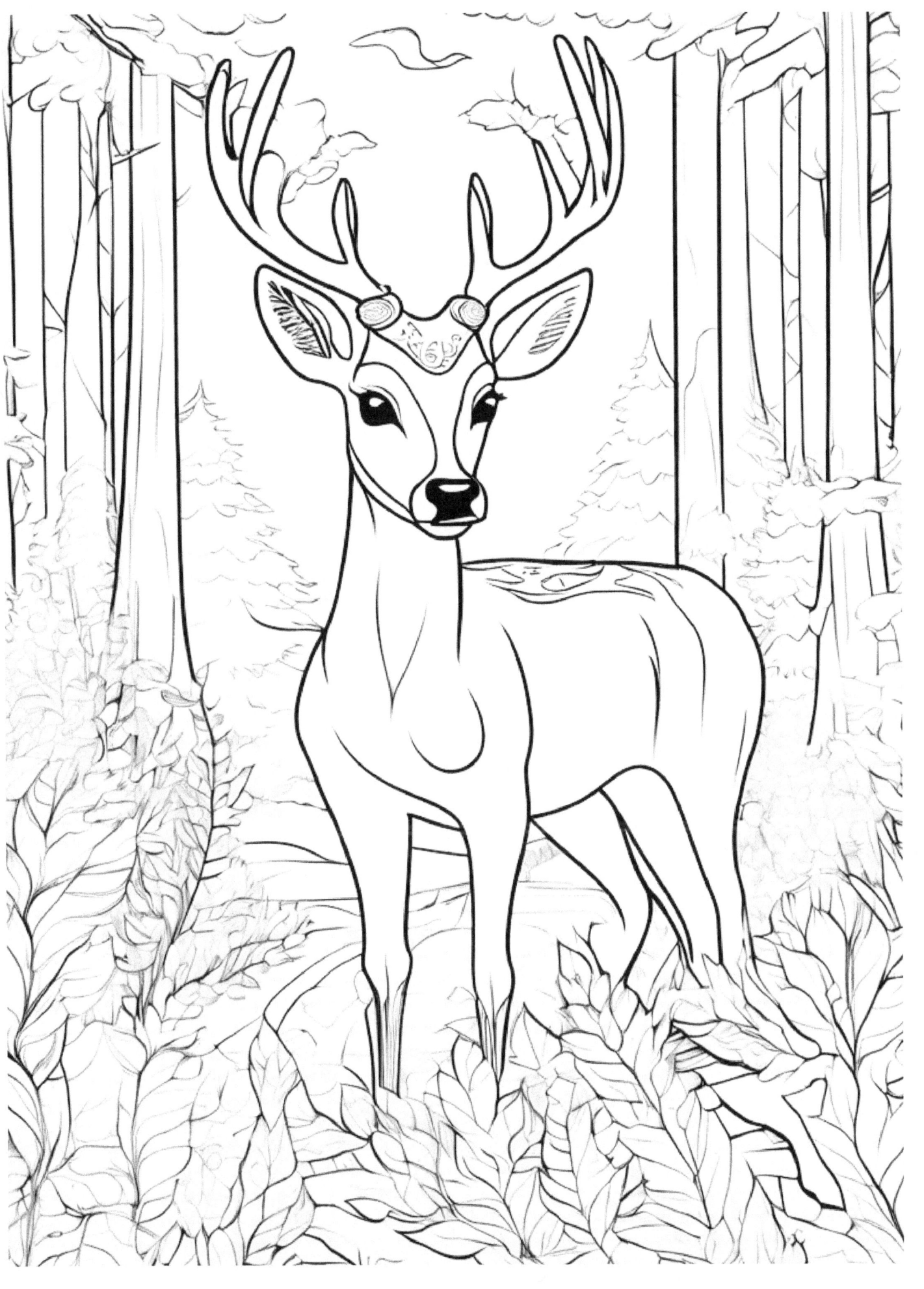

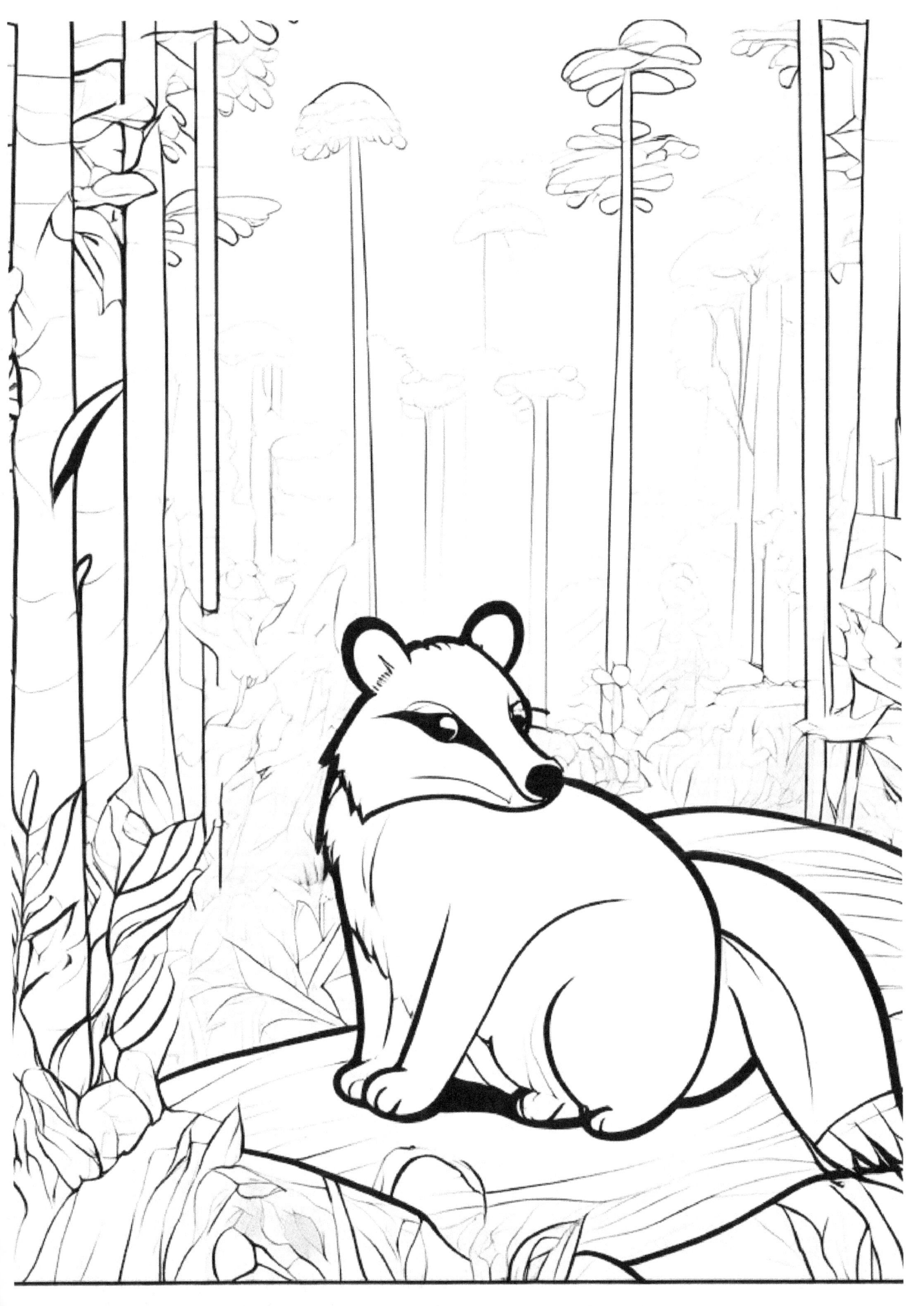

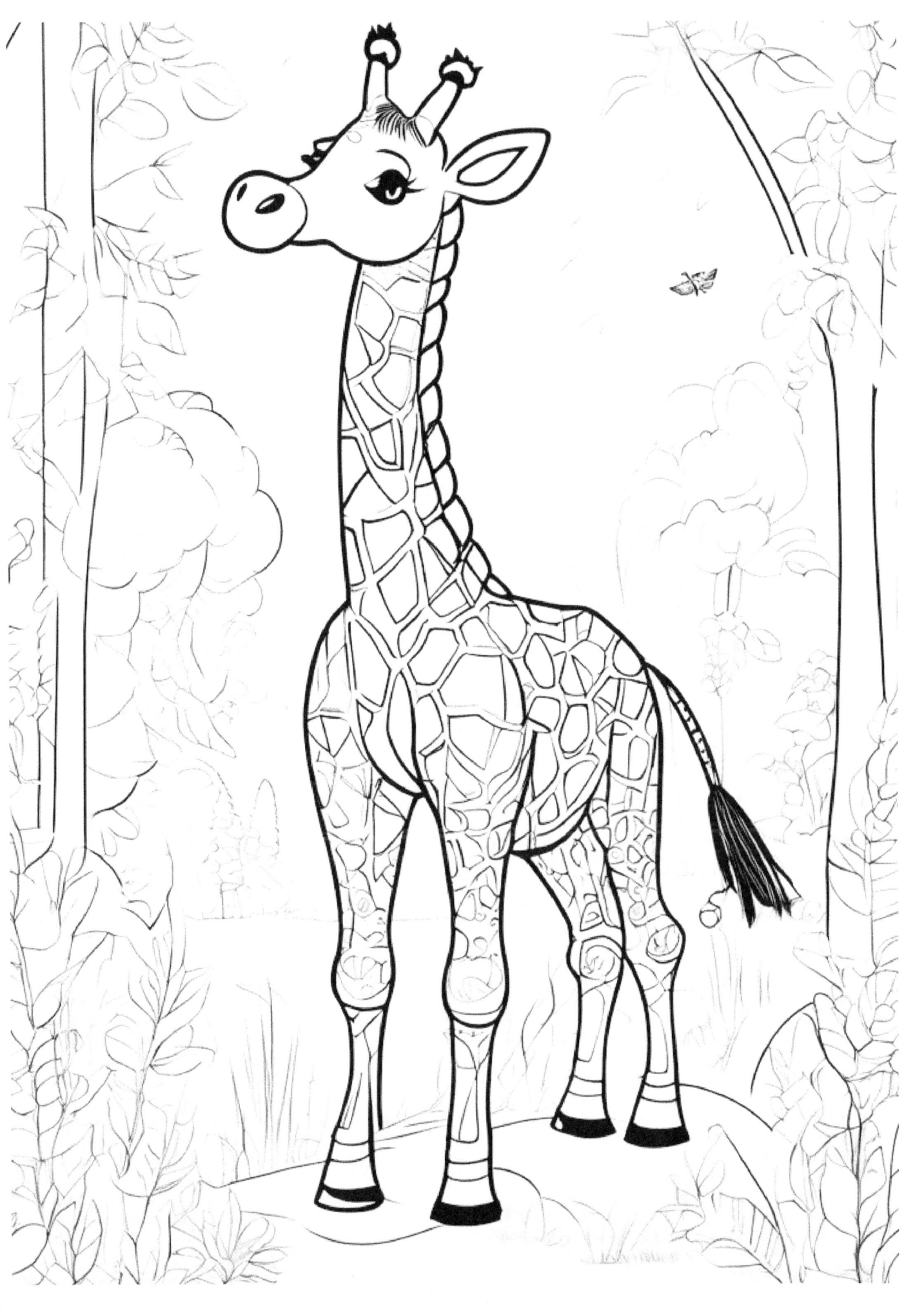

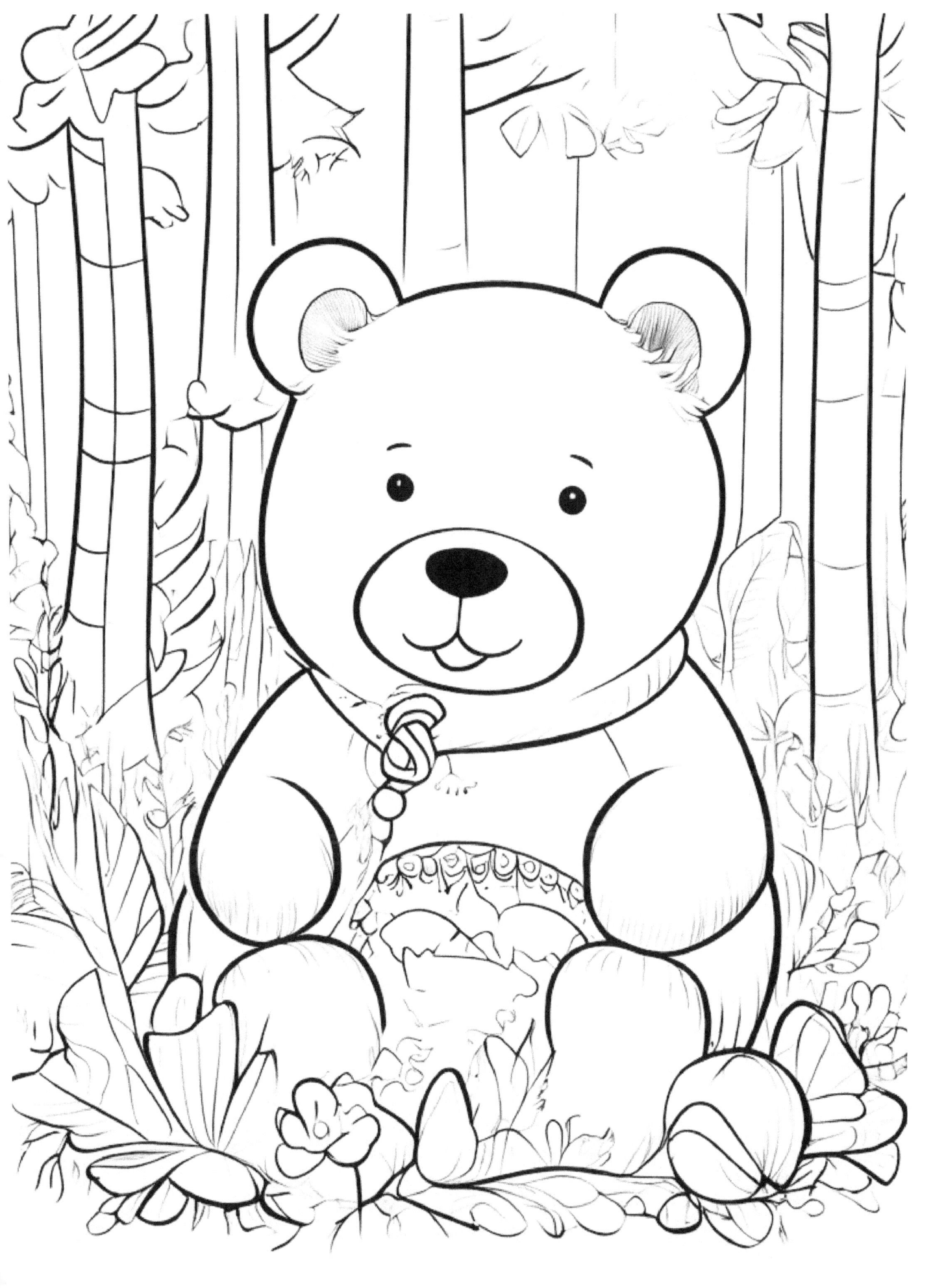

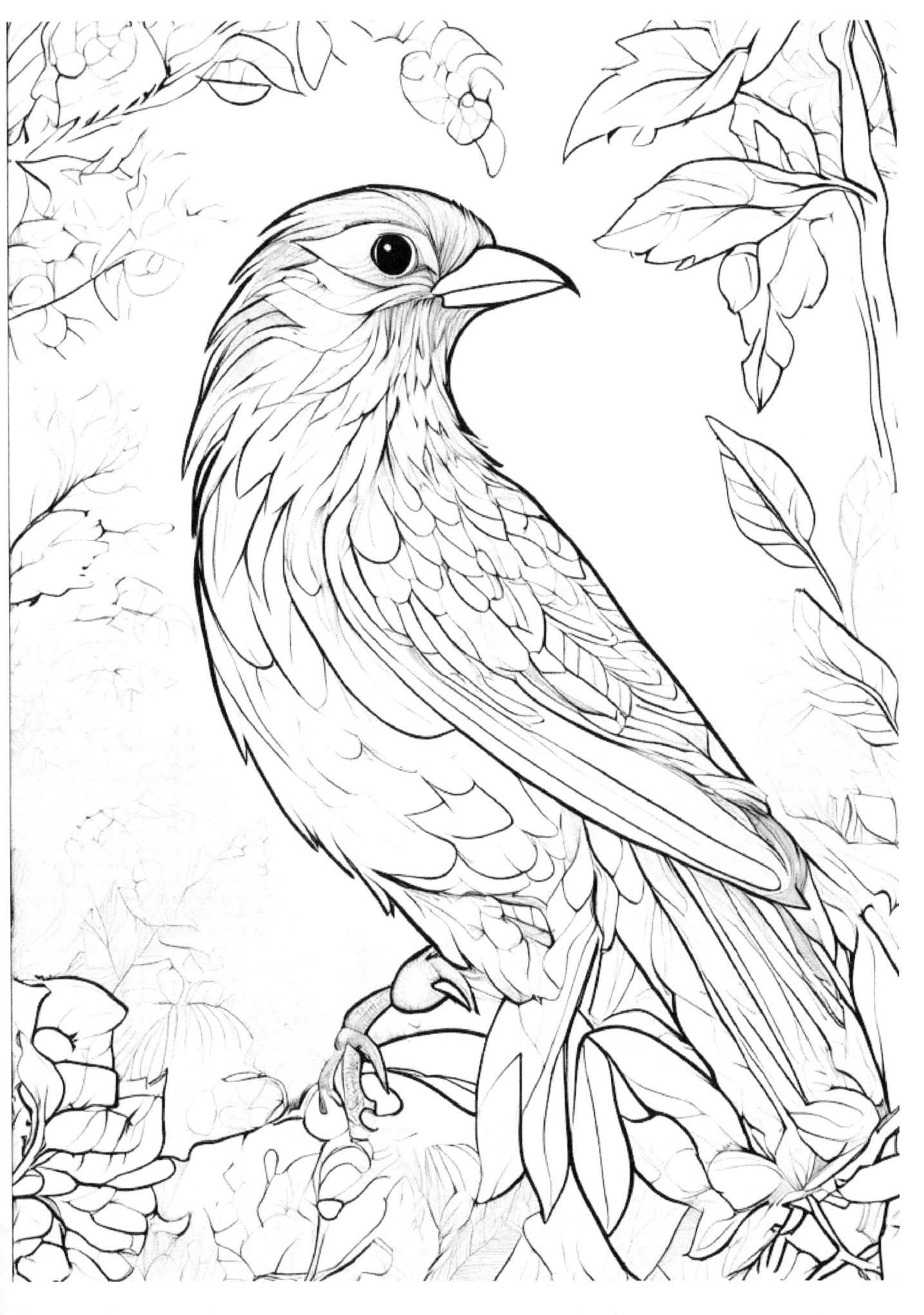

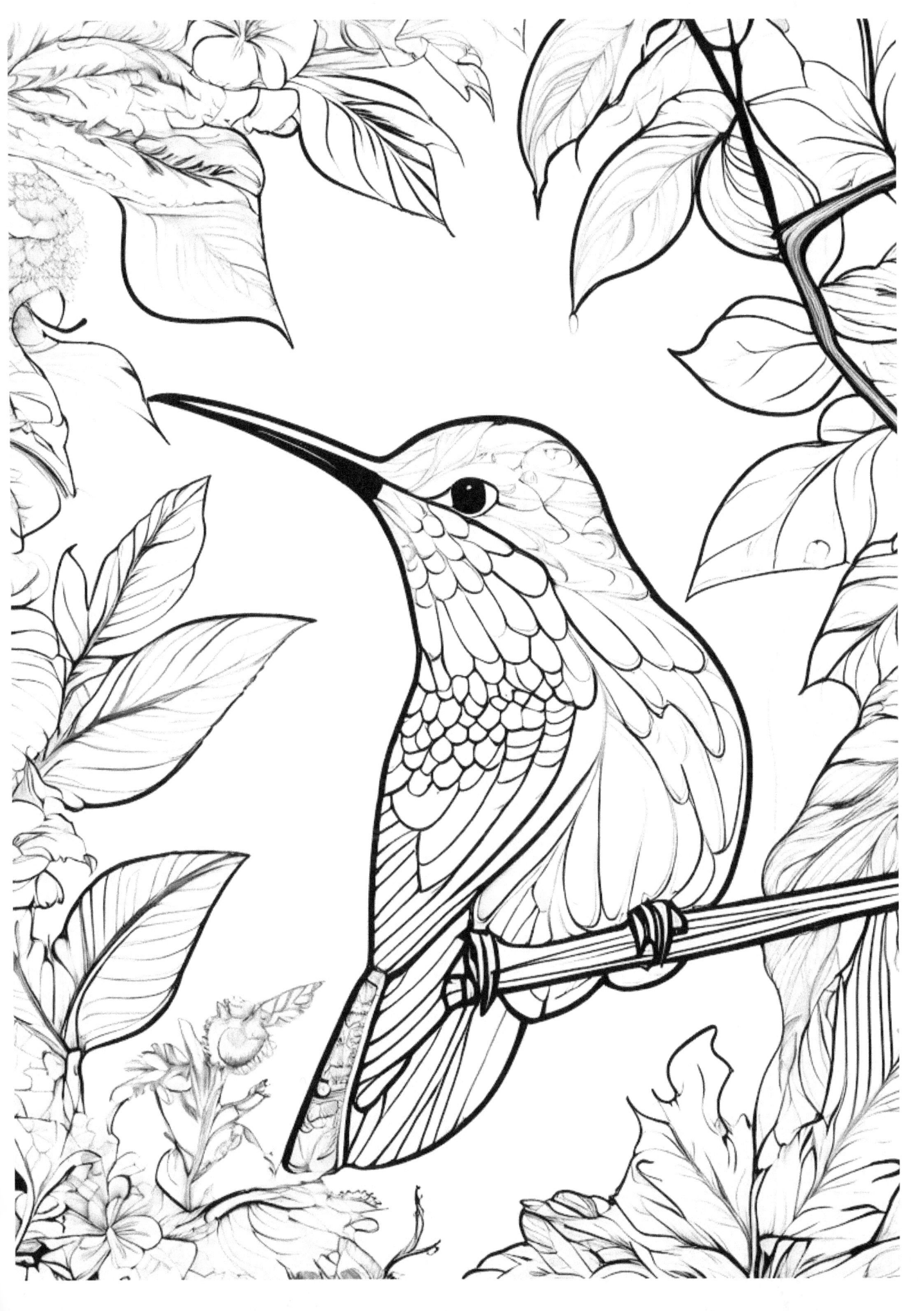

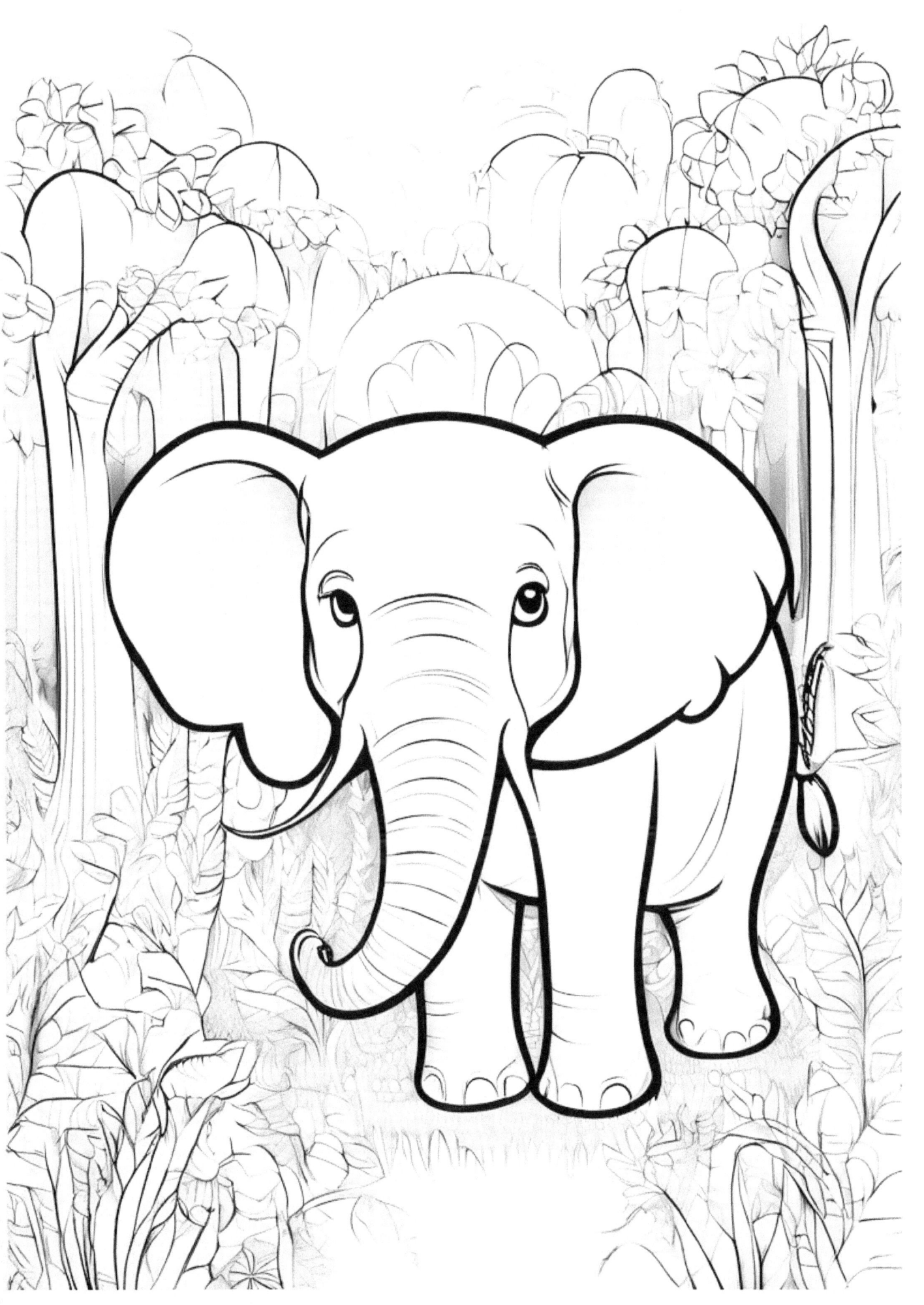

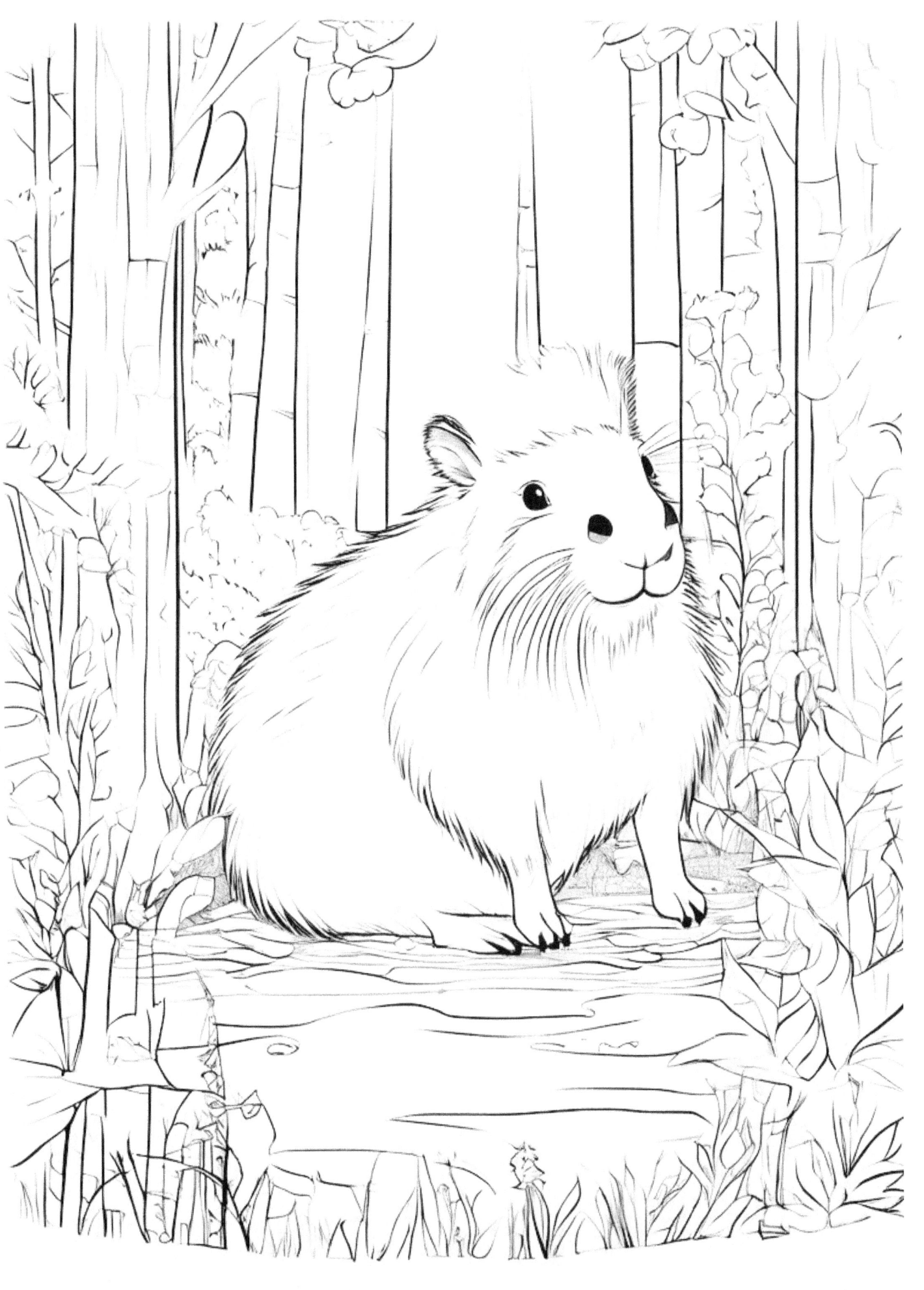

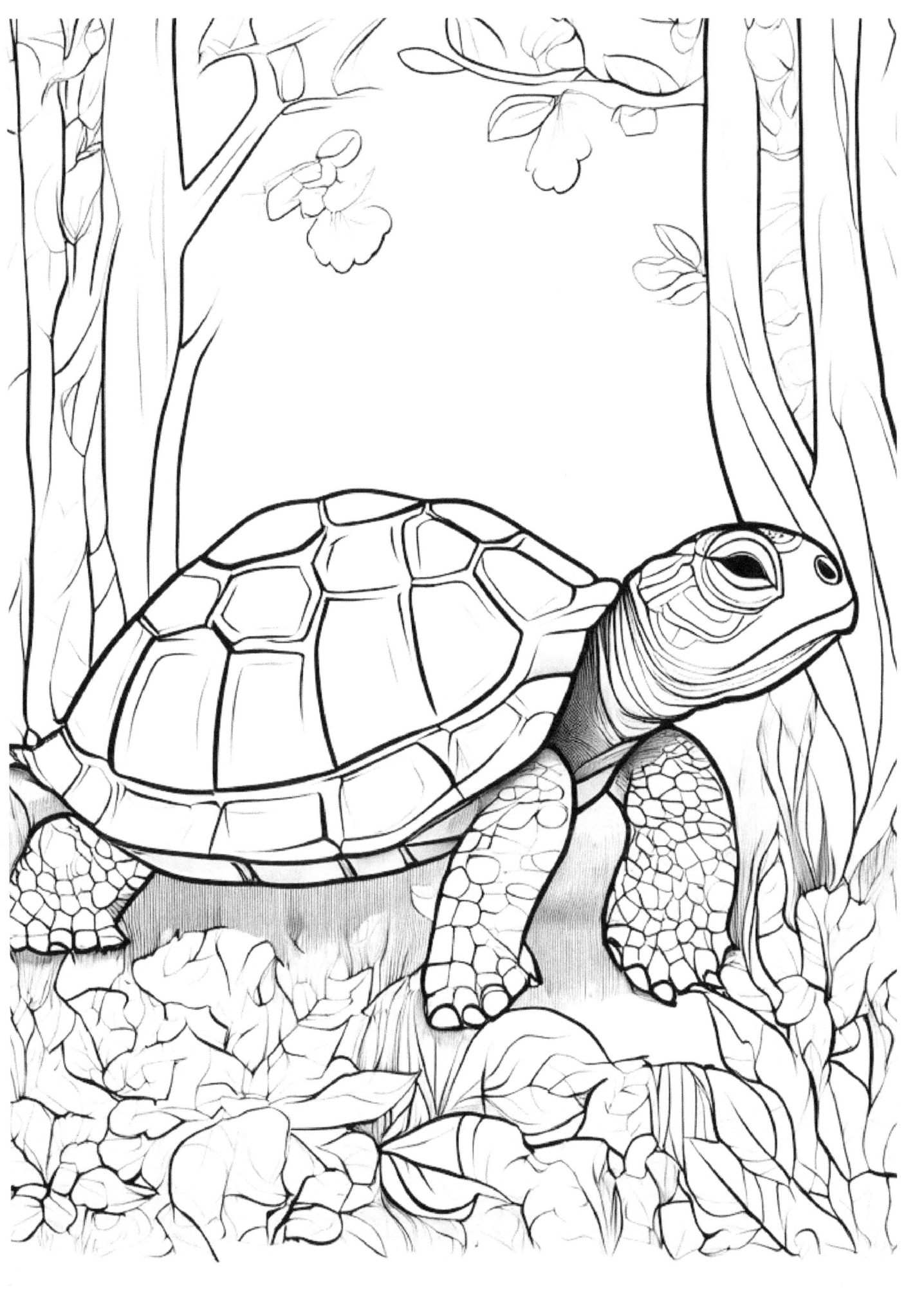

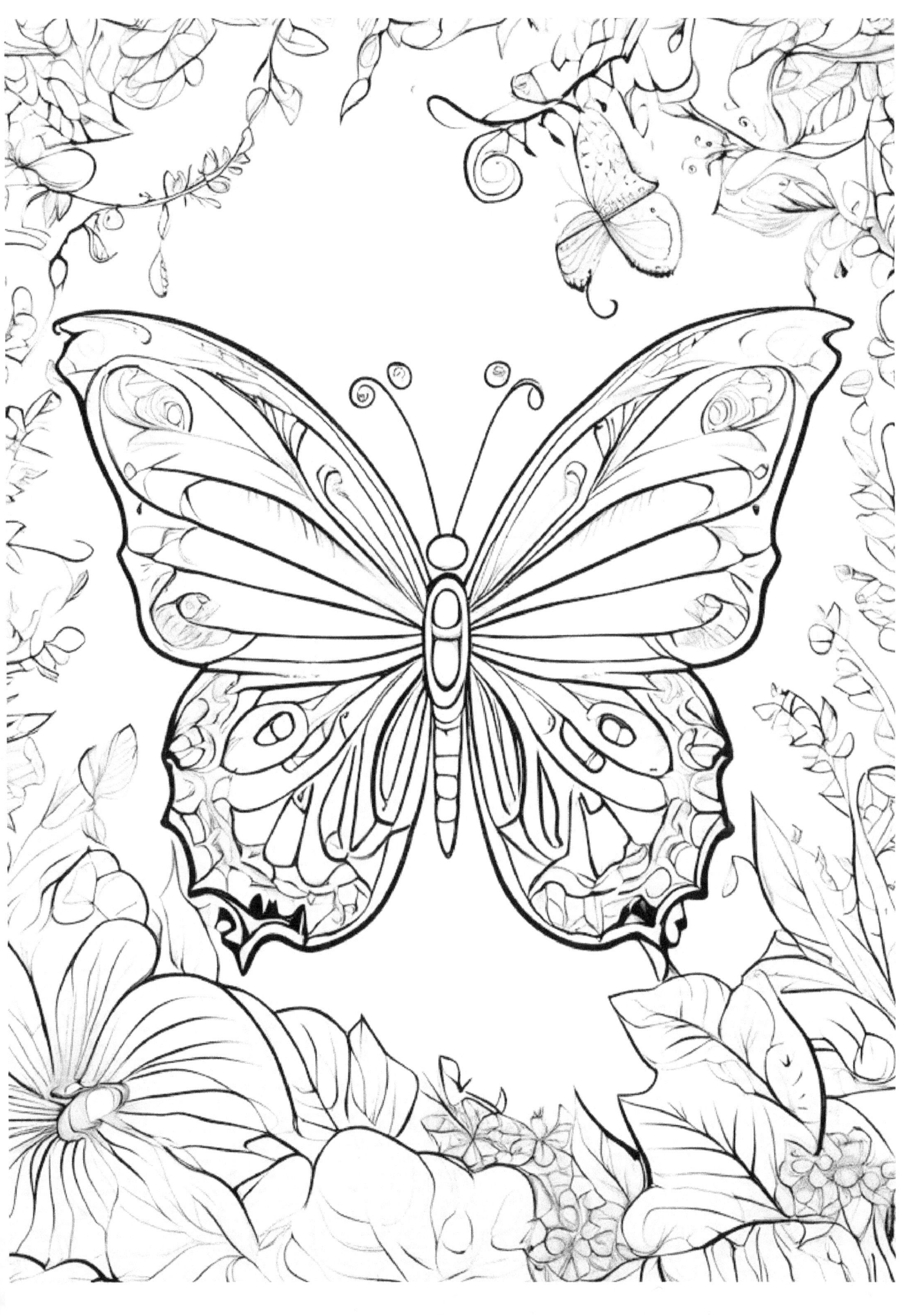

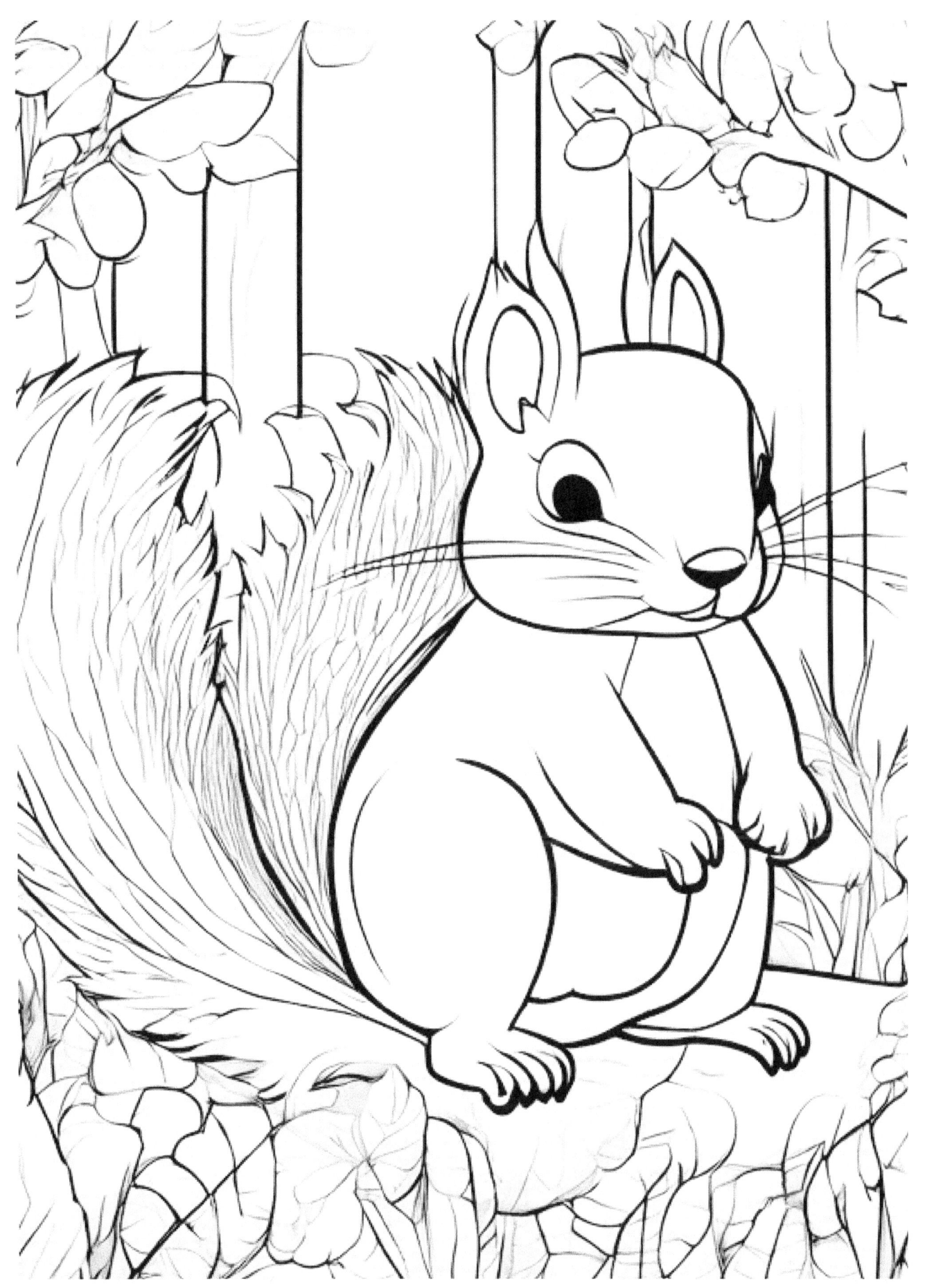

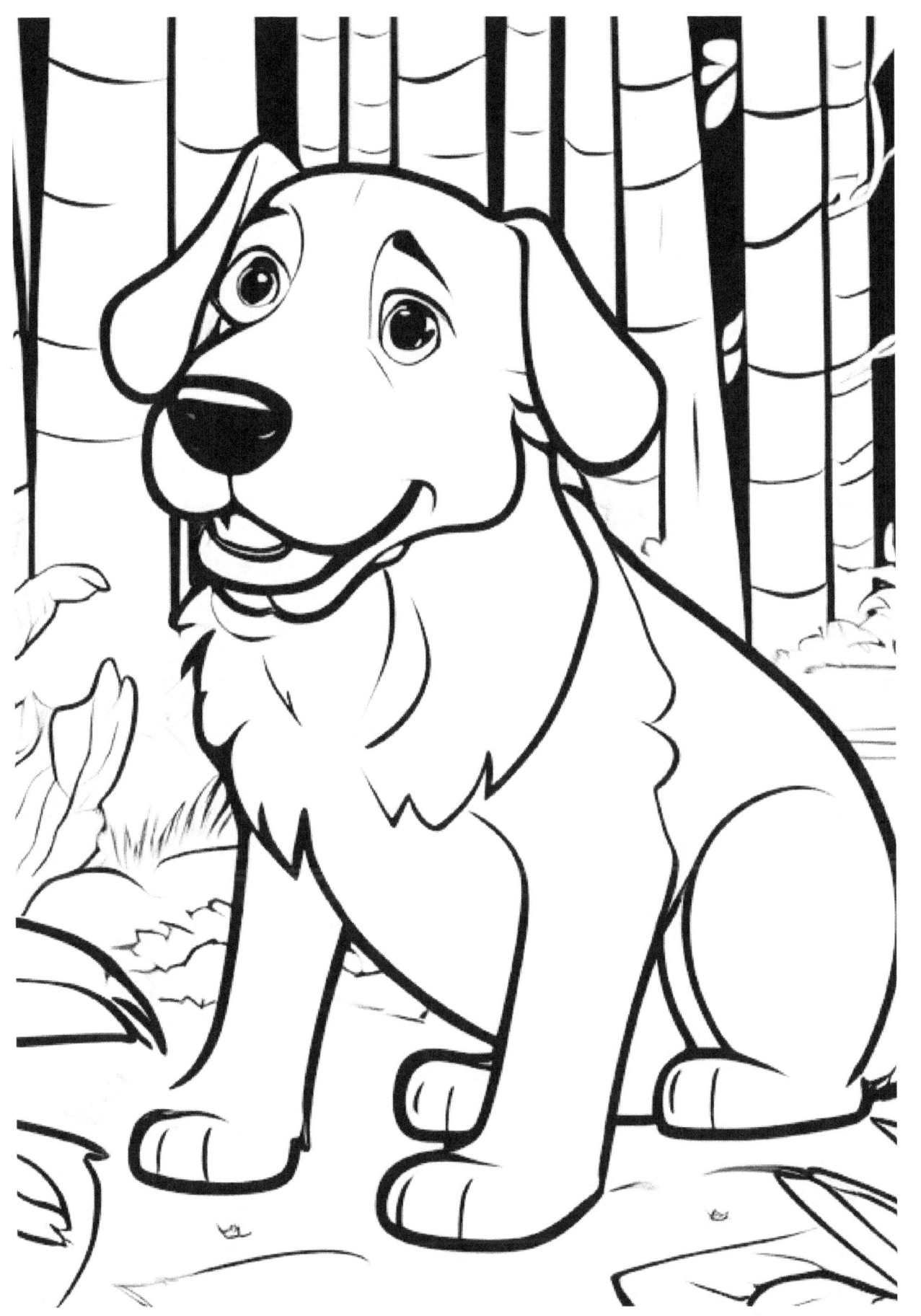

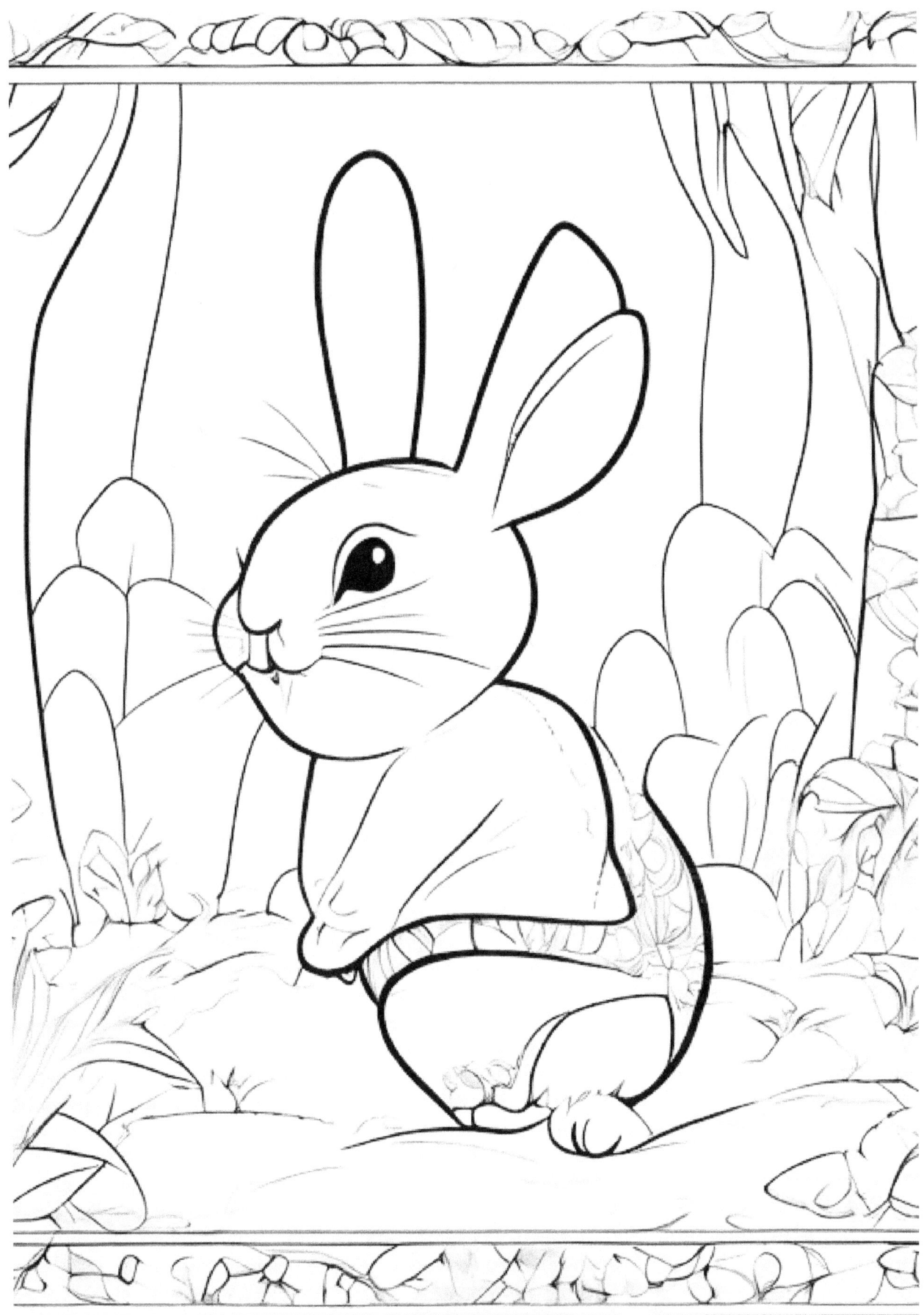

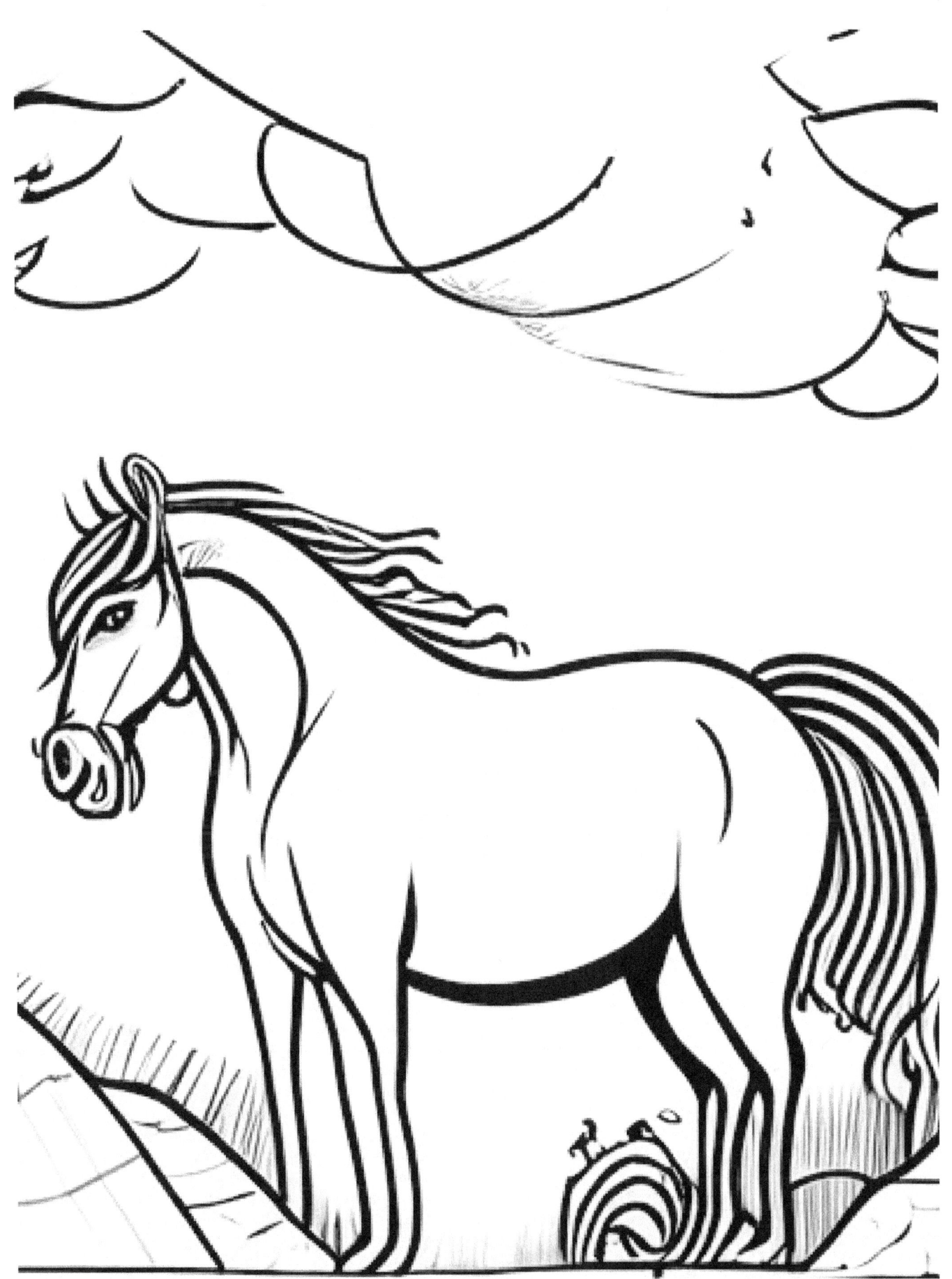

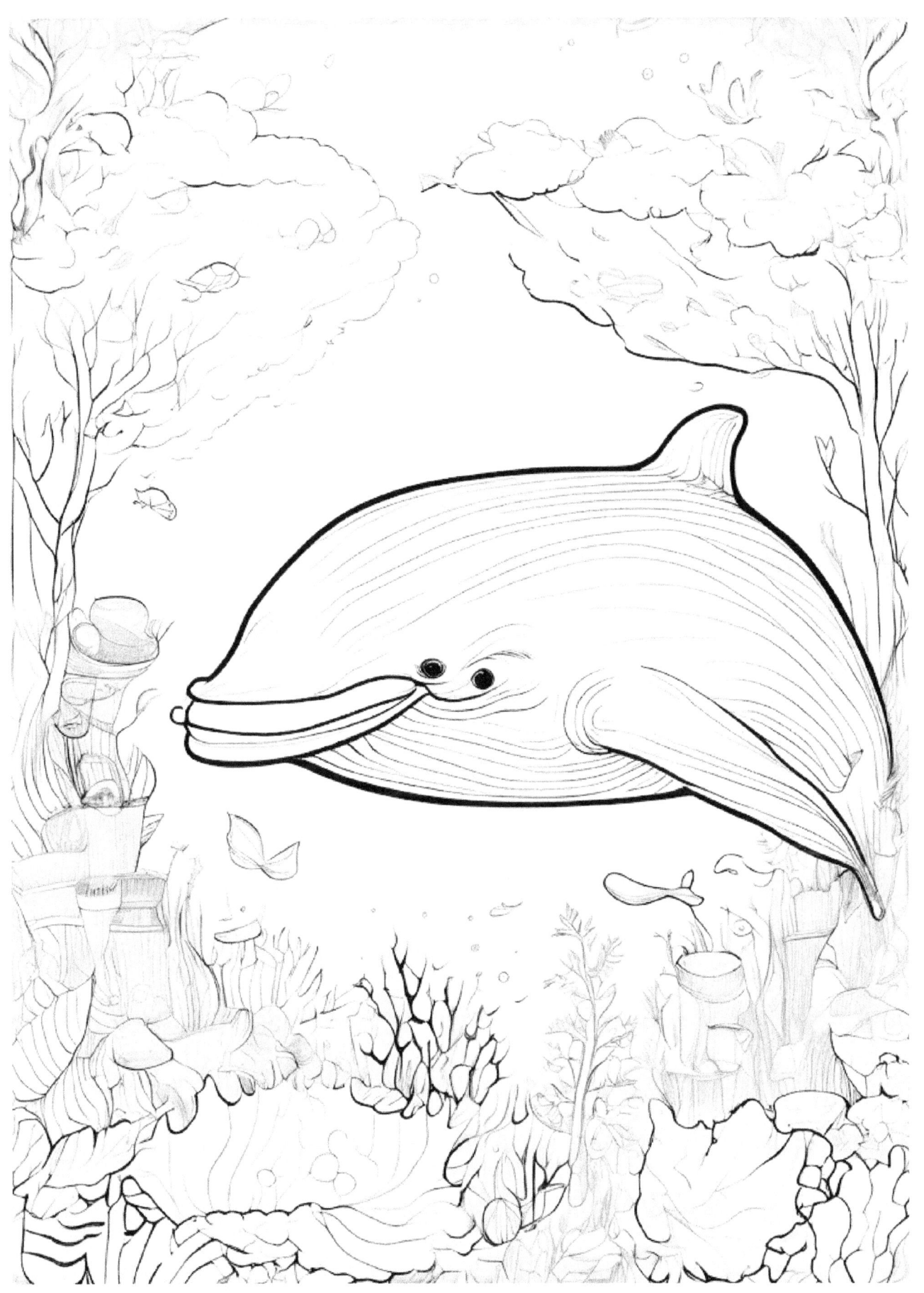

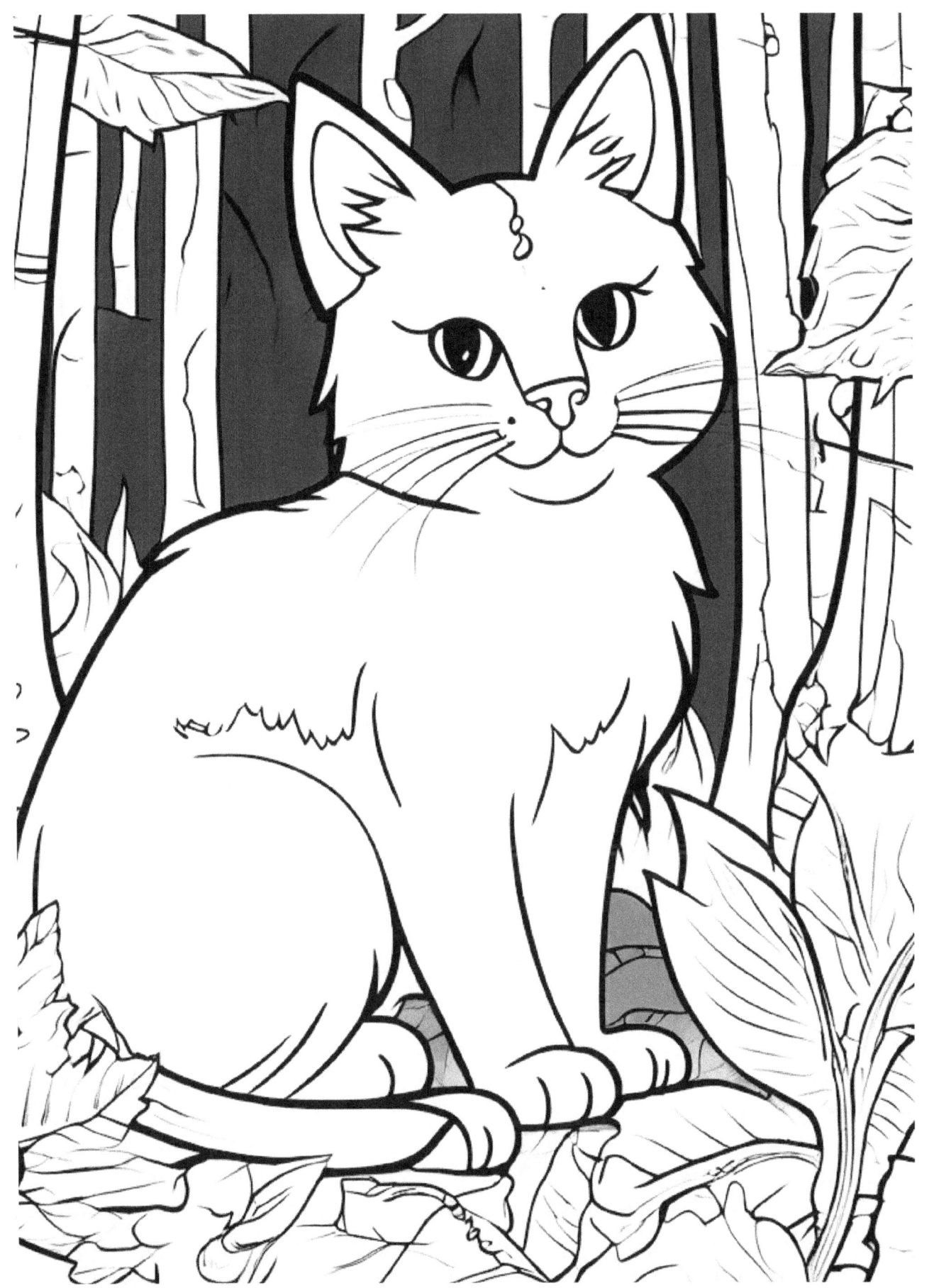

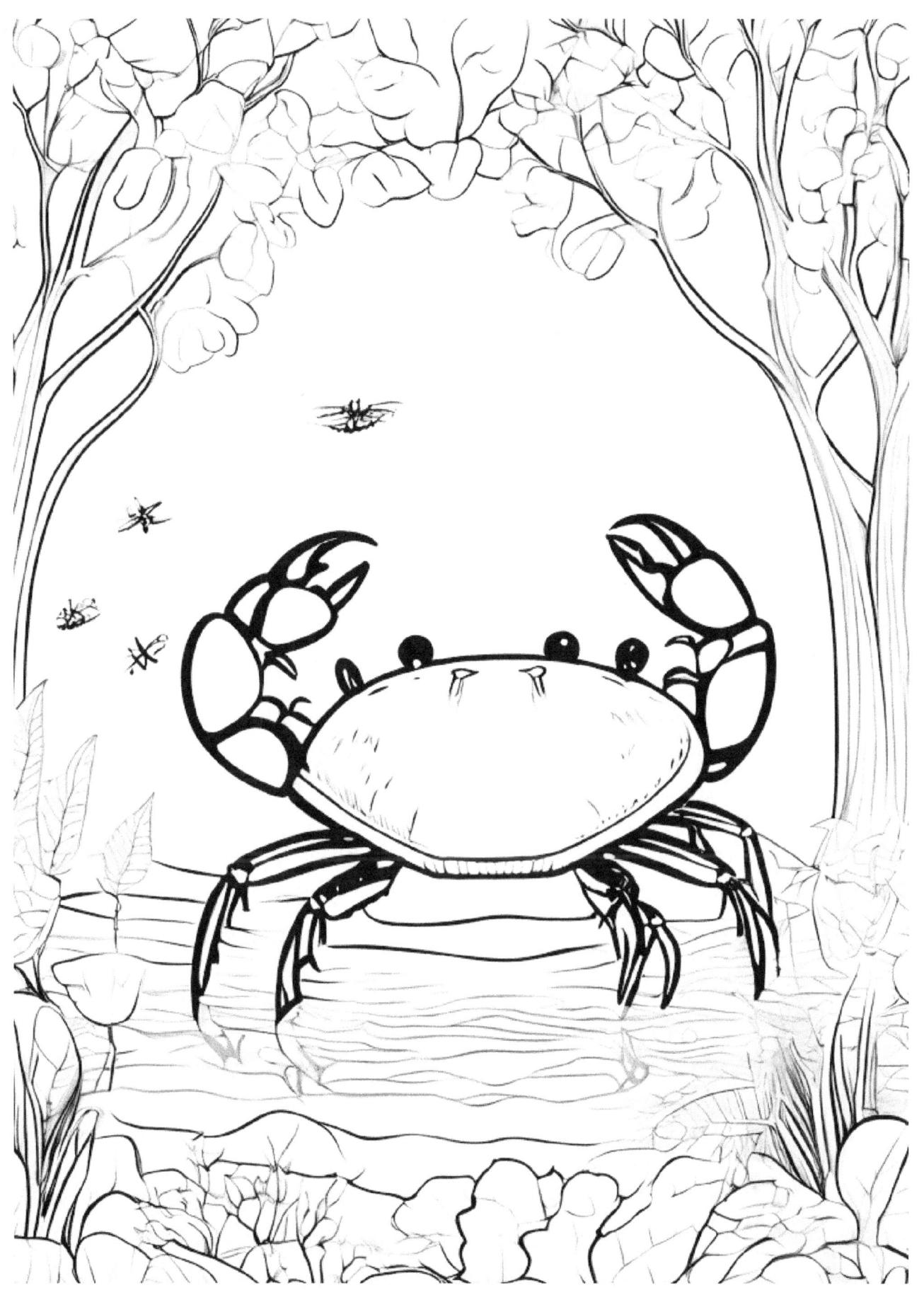

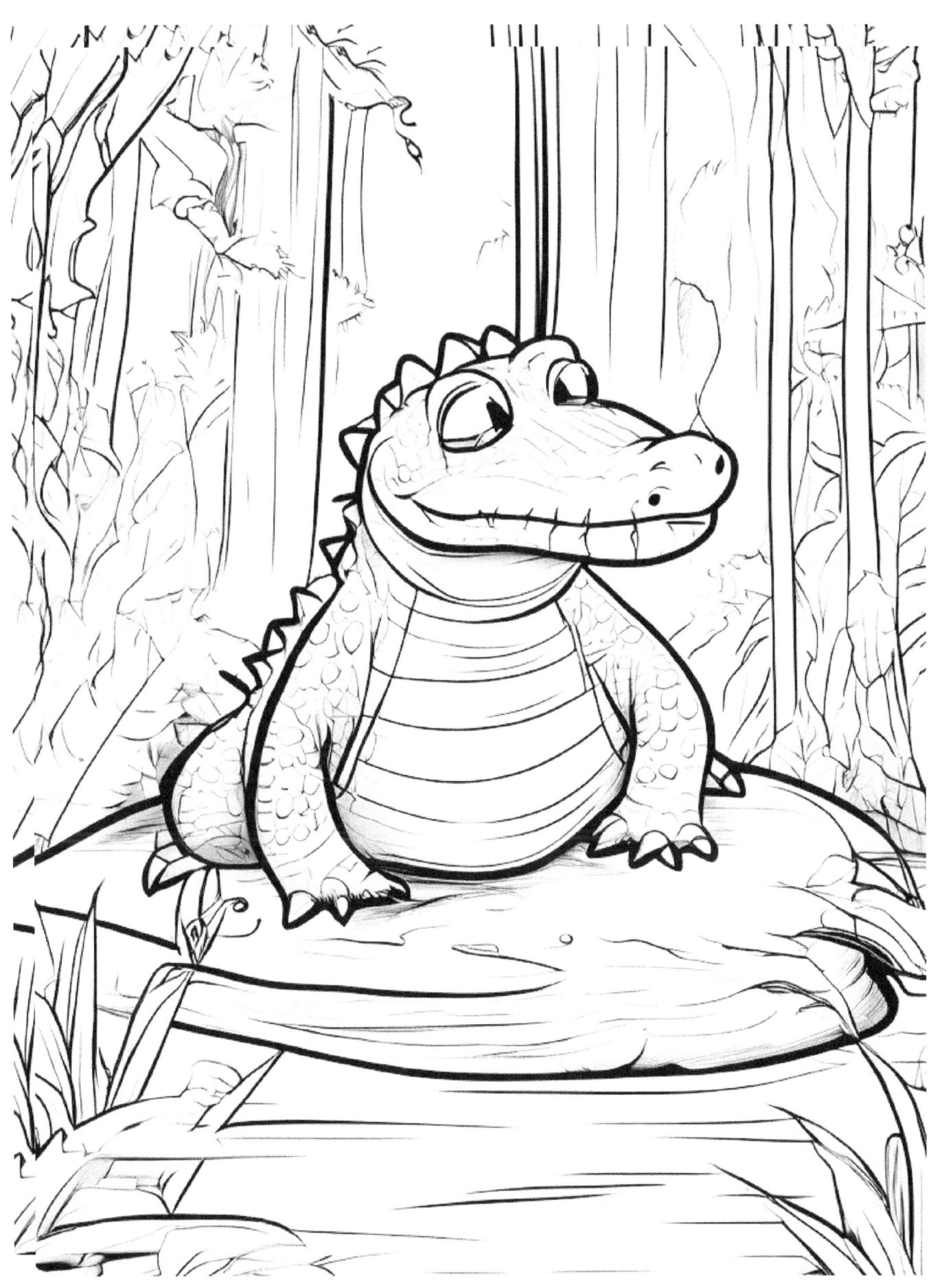

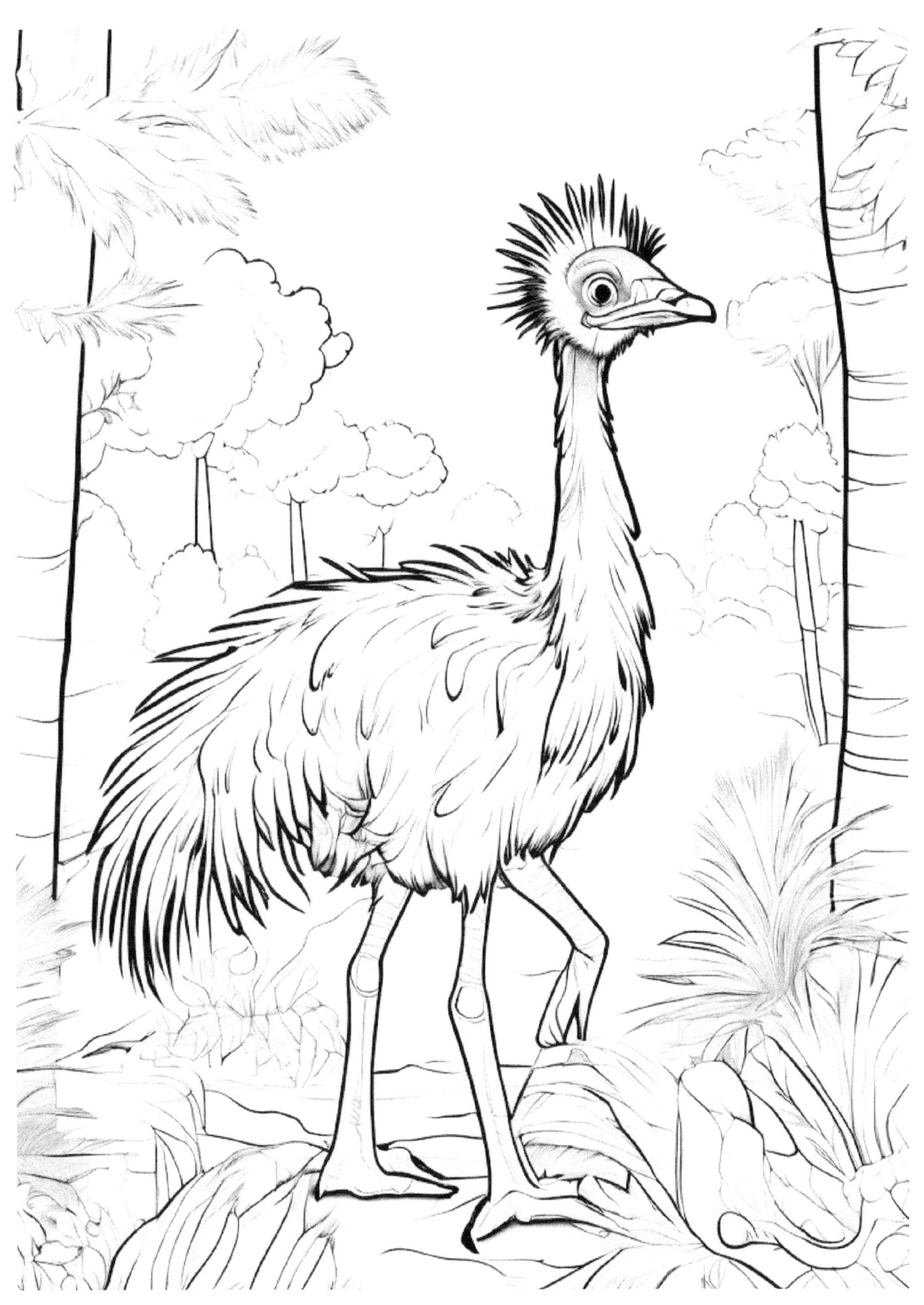

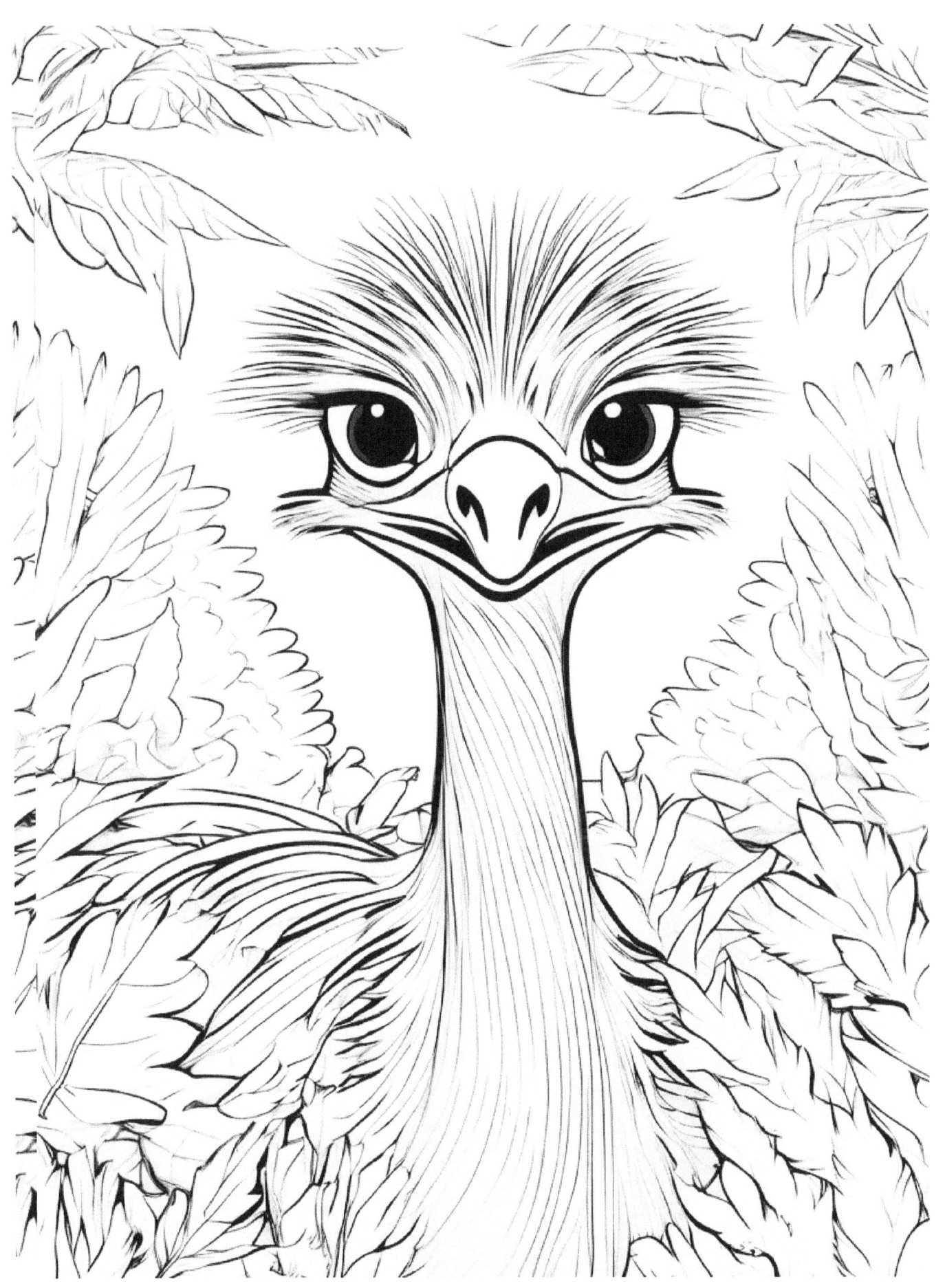

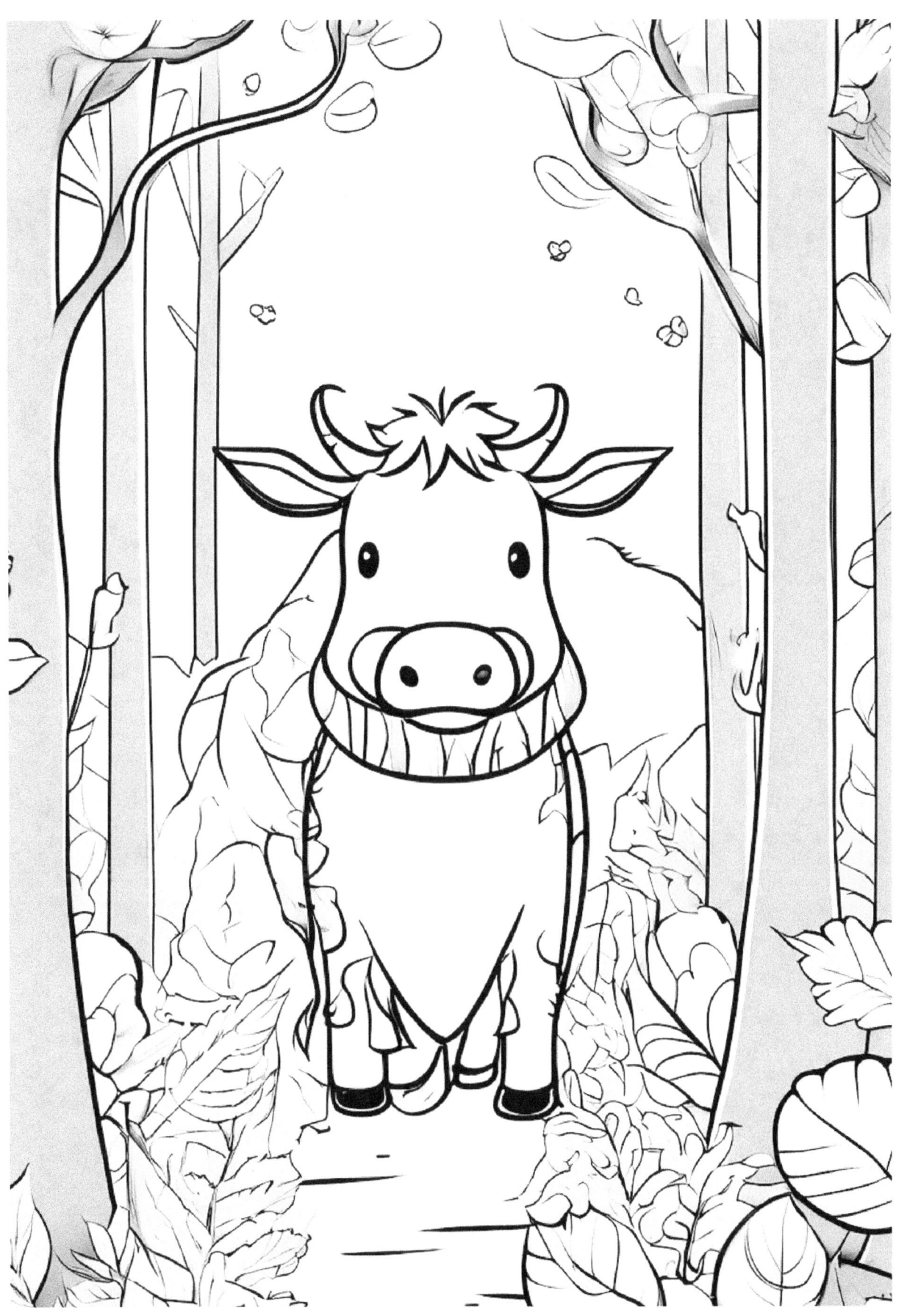

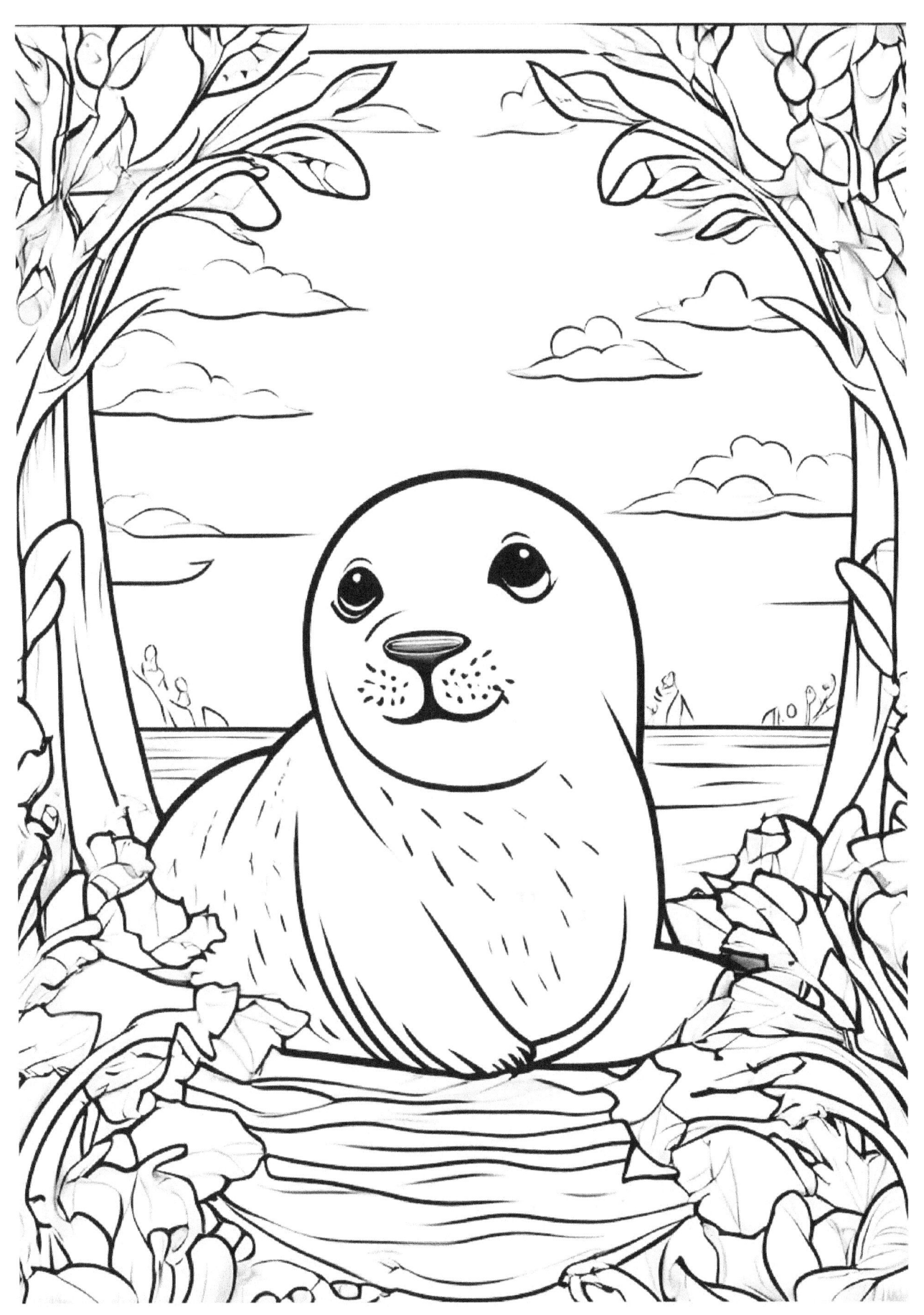

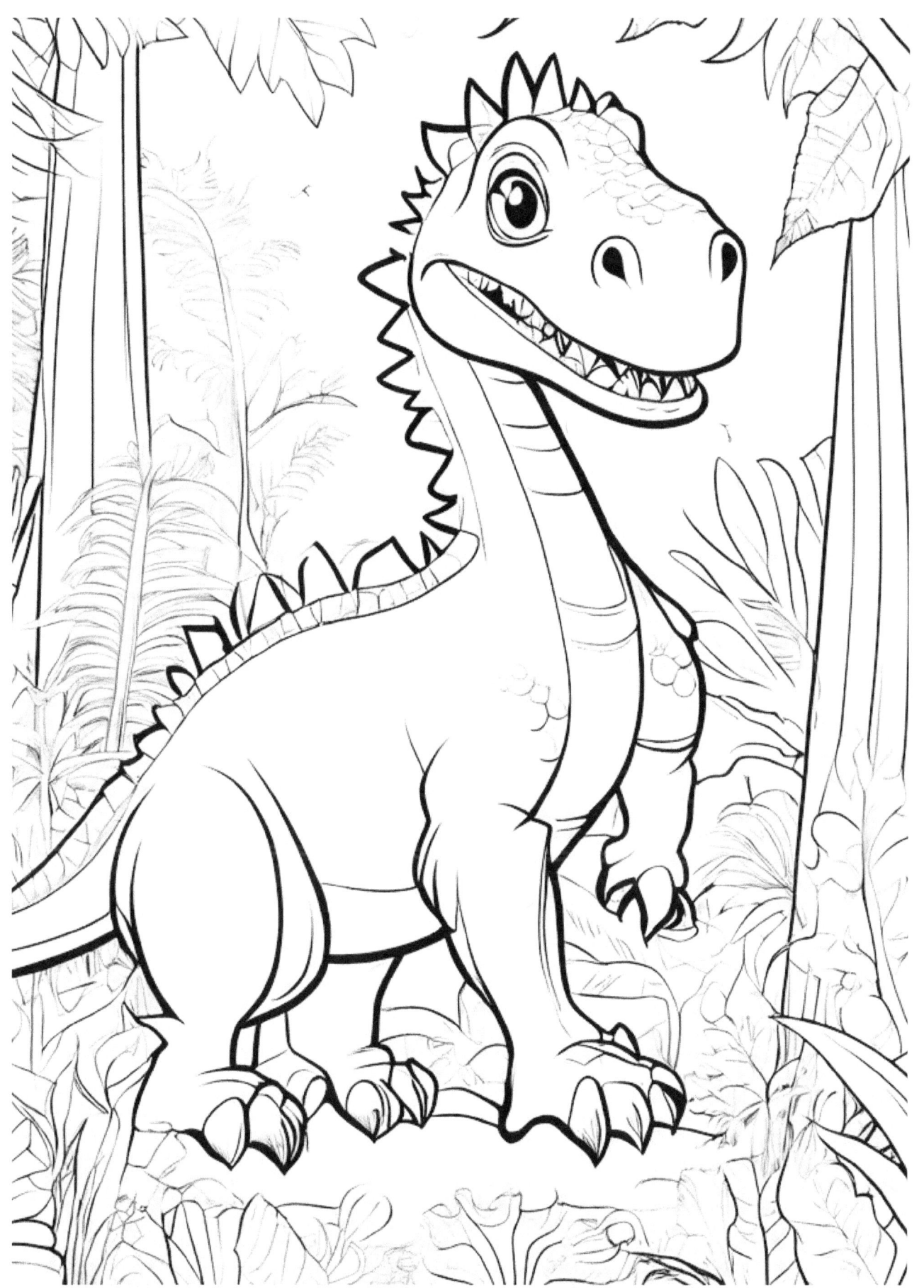

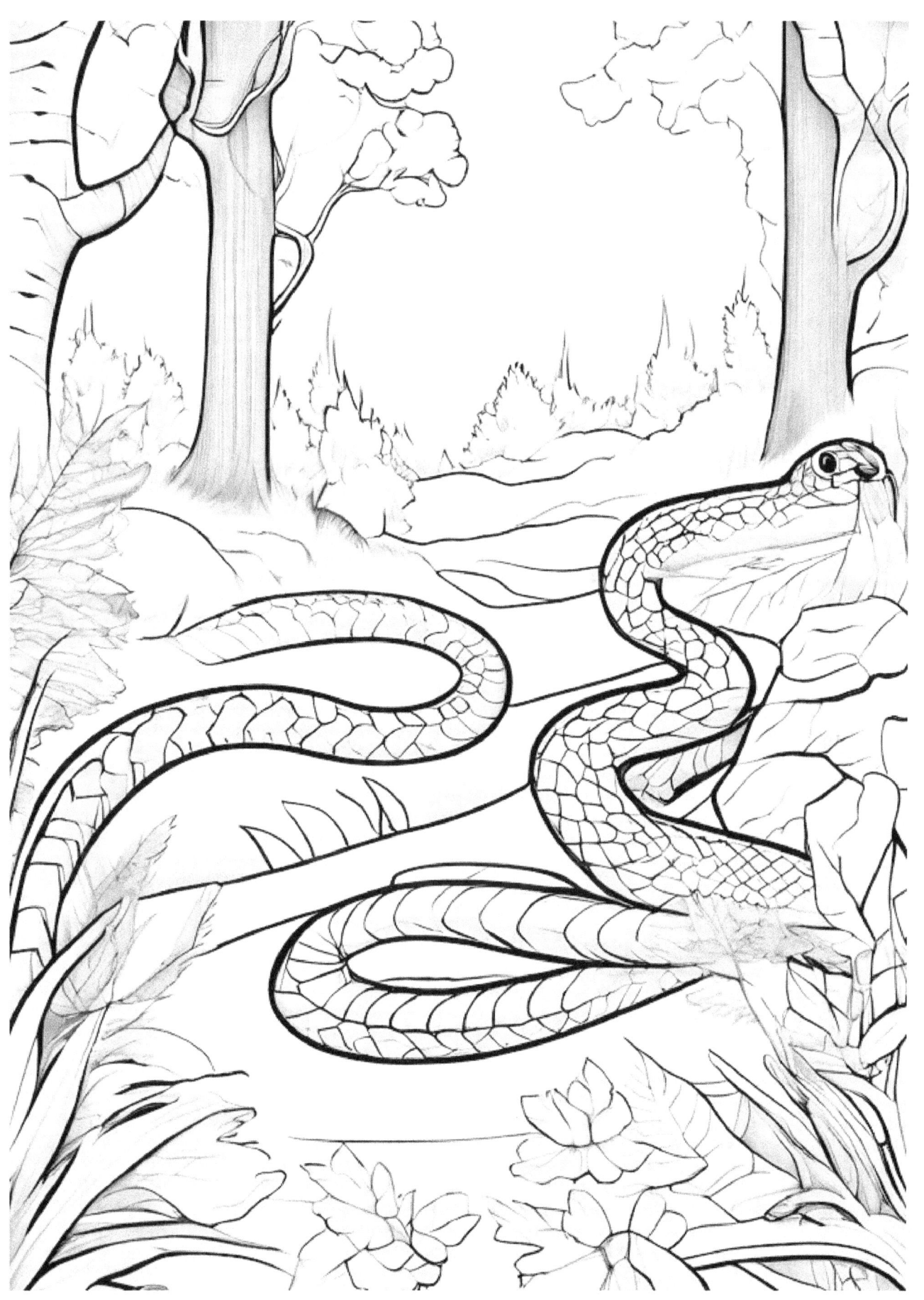

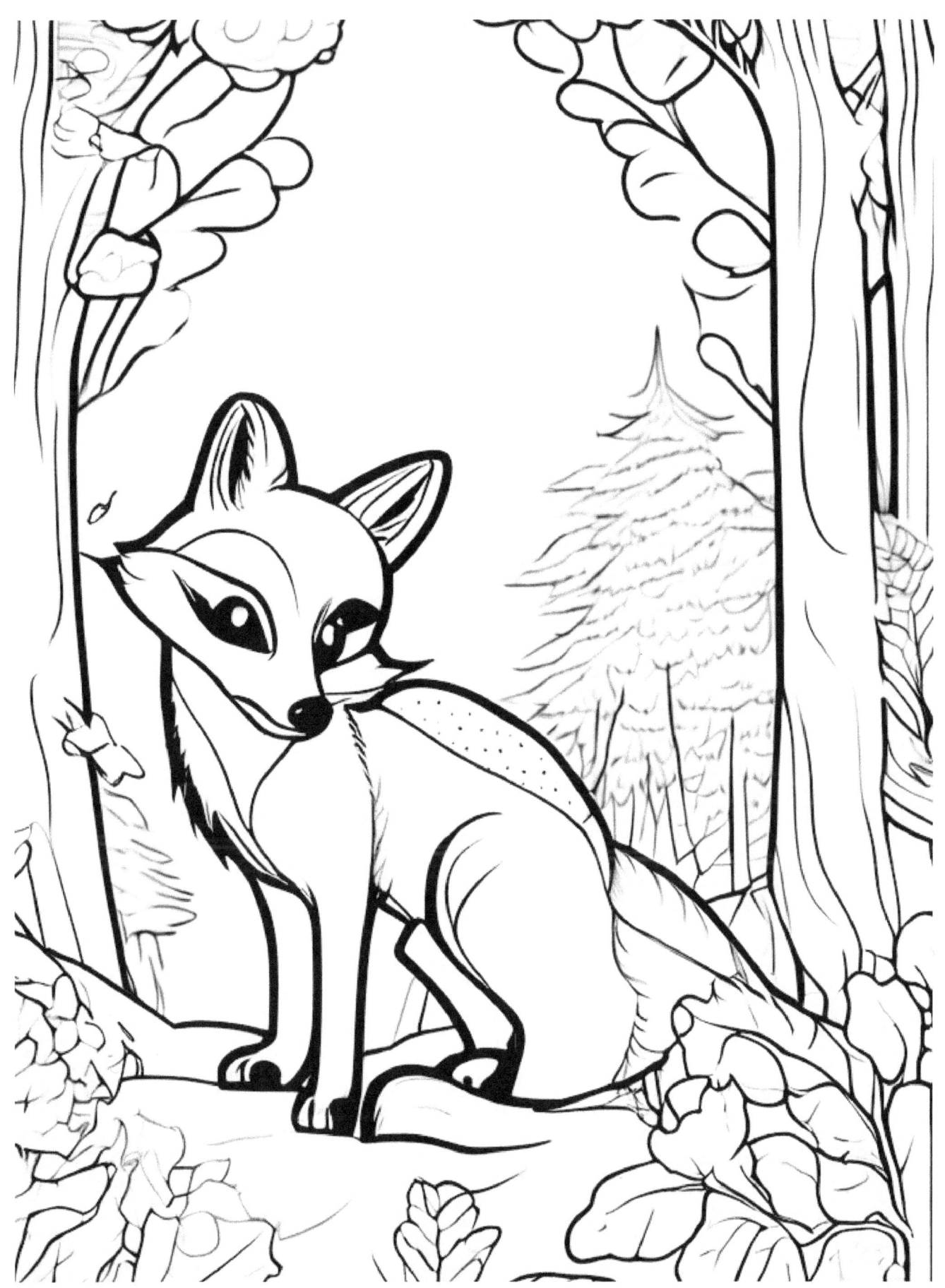

www.ingramcontent.com/pod-product-compliance
Lightning Source LLC
Chambersburg PA
CBHW082219220526
45470CB00010B/3228